*When He Turns
the Page*

About the Author

Tamar says that one of the scriptures she lives by is Jeremiah 29:11, which states: *For I know the thoughts that I think towards you, saith the Lord, thoughts of peace, and not of evil, to give you an expected end.*

She further explains that this scripture was given to her and changes her life daily, and she knows that if her readers place this in their hearts when they think on God their minds will be renewed. It will help people look at life differently. You are not alone!

She loves the Lord and is excited about being in relationship with him. She also writes monthly blogs at TamarDanielle.wordpress.com and hopes to inspire, uplift and encourage many across the world.

When He Turns the Page

Tamar Bradberry

Book Design & Production
Columbus Publishing Lab
www.ColumbusPublishingLab.com

© Tamar Bradberry, 2016
All rights reserved. This book, or parts thereof,
may not be reproduced in any form without permission.

LCCN: 2016945080

Paperback ISBN: 978-1-63337-105-7
E-book ISBN: 978-1-63337-106-4

Printed in the United States of America
1 3 5 7 9 10 8 6 4 2

Contents

My Inspiration	7
The Beginning	9
The Mind is a Terrible Thing to Waste	15
Getting in Where We Fit	18
Insecurities	24
Fear	29
Poem: **Look Beneath**	32
Love vs. Lust	37
As a Body of Christ	48
Back to the Story	49
However...	55
Trials and Tribulations	58
Poem: **Heartfelt**	61
Faith Fighting	62
Poem: **Revealed**	66

Who is He? He is God the father, Son, and Holy Spirit.
He is the author and finisher of my faith.
He is the beginning and the end, the redeemer.
He is the most high, the everlasting God.
He is our father in Heaven!

My Inspiration

In my immaturity I fall. As I mature I stand. I stand upon His word. I stand upon His will, to be separated from myself. I have chosen to follow Christ, His righteousness, even if I stand alone. It is because of Him I lived and because He has shown me and provided me the path, for Him I die.
–Tamar B.

I give honor to my Lord and Savior, Jesus Christ, who is **my motivation, strength and greatest help**. This is dedicated to my immediate family, Mom and Dad, sister and brothers. I love you all, with all my heart, and I've always believed that the first shall be last and the last shall be first. This is just our beginning. I love all my extended family as well! I love you guys from the heart!

I give honor to and I am grateful for Apostle Eddie Perry and Prophetess Melva Perry. I thank you both for your **love and humility and honor** in the Lord. Thank you for being examples and helping me at my weakest moments by the spirit of God. I love you whole heartedly and I cherish you both. **Great things!**

The purpose of this book is to provide insight from a woman to other women and younger girls. My hope is that this book will encourage, uplift and help women understand their **value and worth** and overcome their battle. Men can also read it to gain knowledge because men also go encounter these experiences in life. This book entails my journey and how I grew to **overcome** these obstacles. My prayer is that whoever reads this book will gain **understanding** throughout seasons of life, and that they will become enlightened about who they are and how they navigate life in their thinking and choices. **Every day matters**. I hope to inspire you and that you will allow me to take you on this journey. Are you ready? **Turn the page!** You are not alone! Love you. We all go through battles throughout life.

The Beginning

The struggle between self-identity and who others wanted me to be was far too overwhelming and confusing after the age of nine. I was the type of young girl who loved the smell of the air, the wind blowing through my hair and the sun beaming on my face. Everything about the outside was beautiful to me. I was often called weird by most, but perhaps I was just extremely shy. I grew up in a Christian household.

I was the only child conceived in Columbus, Ohio. The other three siblings were born in Mobile, Alabama. My dad always called me the buckeye. It made me feel sad in a way because I wanted to be from Alabama also. If it isn't obvious, my father and mother are from Alabama. My mother is so bashful and my dad is outgoing. They journeyed to Columbus, Ohio for a change of scenery. My family growing up wasn't perfect, but in my eyes we were. I remember there was a season in life in our young age when behaviors, attitudes, and demeanors shifted like never before. Looking back, I am glad that I have experienced this **journey** because my family has come a long way.

As I mentioned I am not the only child—I have two brothers and one sister who are all older than me. My siblings and I are all stair stepped in age. Who I am today and many of the things I have done were learned, and some genetically coded from DNA. Growing up I was extremely shy—shy to the point where I would hide behind my mother's leg and smile at everything. Growing up was very interesting and fun. Time seems like it moved very slowly as a kid. As a kid I was into all kinds of fun sports and loved to draw, dance and write, as were my siblings. My parents kept us very close; **we were each other's protectors** and we also annoyed each other. Well, I guess you can say that the older two had to look after the younger two. I remember when my dad caught me doing the butterfly, I got in so much trouble. I didn't know what the dance was, I saw it on TV and mimicked it. I was forewarned not to do so again. Of course, I did not listen. I was a kid.

My siblings and I were so tight that when you messed with one, you messed with all. We took up for each other at all costs. My mother was and still is **the pillar of the family**. She is the glue, the nurturer, the giver, and her heart is pure as gold, but she is also feisty. So funny. I think it's where I get it from. What she has done for my siblings and me, I can never thank her enough for stretching herself. **Mom, you have my heart and always will.**

My dad, he's so passionate, warm, heartfelt, he is also the rock, the heartbeat, the strength and most courageous—he's said to be a sharp shooter when it comes to the gospel, lol. My dad also has the **purest heart,** and when my parents cry—my God, there is a stream that flows that reminds me of **God's love**. My dad was a preacher and currently still preaches. I remember when we were kids we were in the living room every night practicing the Lord's Prayer and singing gospel songs. He made sure we got it down. I even remember when he would give us lectures about something that we may have gotten in trouble for, but it turned into a sermon. It was so funny because we would fall asleep and he would wake us back up. He was still preaching as if we were the congregation. Memories!

I love my mother and father and siblings so dearly. I am glad we are all close and we carry each other as believers to resist the things that cause hindrances in our lives. Although my parents aren't together anymore—they divorced when I was at a young age—my dad has never left my life. **No one is**

left behind. As we grew older, we all resubmitted our lives to Christ with new knowledge and understanding, and we are now **walking in the order of the Lord**. Everyone makes mistakes, but it's how you finish that matters, and the best finish is getting in **relationship with God** and maturing in your understanding by the word of God. Today my dad and mom are beautiful people in Christ and so are my siblings. What the devil means for evil, **God turns for your good**.

As I reached my early twenties, my family and my fellowship with the church kept me spiritually grounded, and I have been walking in Christ faithfully since the age of twenty-three. I used to battle hard with myself for a long time, and it was the constant prayers and struggles of family who kept me surviving in the midst of my destruction. The thing was, I knew what I wanted, I knew that I was meant to do something, and I knew that there was something greater for me. Where I was **before Christ** came fully in my life was a place I never wanted to be. At the time I didn't know how to detach myself from my surroundings. It wasn't until God made me extremely exhausted with the life I was living that I went seeking more of His presence. We all get asked the question, what would we do differently if we had the chance? But I realize the past is the past and I can't do anything but improve and build my future.

I share this short introduction to say to you, like many

of us who think we are alone considering how we grew up or the things we faced, there is a **commonality** somewhere in our stories. Depending on the surroundings of any cultural environment, we create habits and disciplines that are hard to break. Whether you face abandonment, heartbreak, suffering, loneliness, fear, or hardness of the heart, my desire is to encourage you to **fight through**. It's possible to overcome these things.

I would like to share with you my journey. The journey is never ending. There is a solution in finding out who you are, even when society attempts to mold you to weaken your mental ability to keep you trapped. The solution? I found who I was when I gave my life to Jesus. **I became free.** This is only the beginning of the journey on which you are about to embark. Become uplifted, encouraged and inspired. Know **you aren't alone** and that God's about to...

Turn the page!

THE MIND IS A TERRIBLE THING TO WASTE

I start with the mind because it is the most primary thing that we fight with on a day to day basis. You have to understand that the mind isn't just natural, but **spiritual** as well. The mind constantly thinks and generates information. It's where we store our emotions, reactions, thoughts and many other things.

I've had a great conscious awareness of the operation of my mind ever since I was a little girl. I used to create stories and scenarios of fairytale relationships. I always saw things in a positive light until I experienced a life of heartache and disappointment. I grew cold after my first experience with what I saw as an opportunity of a relationship. In my mind I started to build that fairytale I had created in my head. I was young and naive and really didn't comprehend reality.

After my first relationship in middle school, I experienced heartbreak twice. So many emotions caved in, and I realized appearances didn't matter, being nice or good to people didn't matter. I was emotionless and I had a plan to hate and to break those who were in my way. My emotions told my mind to destroy those who hurt me. Don't get me wrong, I didn't walk around cruel; I was a sweetheart who was very nice and giving. But certain situations triggered certain emotions.

Regardless of how I treated others—men in particular—I would always try to rationalize with myself, but I continuously built up **a wall in my heart** toward the opposite sex. However, my relationship with females was such that I would befriend them very closely as if they were my family, and when they hurt me I still loved them past that. One would think my reaction toward my friends would have been the same, but I was very forgiving of my friends. There was one similar thing I saw that we all had, and that was in reference to our perceptions of life—we were all broken inside from something we experienced. All of our lives had **missing pieces** that another's life had, which filled the void. How we thought and our perceptions of certain things were immature.

I learned my deepest resentment was toward men only because of a couple encounters I previously had. I find it very interesting how subconsciously without noticing the human mind can subliminally rate itself as the victim. As maturity sets in, I recognize that we have several ways of thinking—we could rationalize, or think positive/negative. The mind could imagine and turn situations into things that never happened, as well as perceptions that lead to wrong thinking. I learned that the things the mind was doing I could later control with my very own responses to myself.

I would have never known these things had it not been for the **word of God** and the **Holy Spirit** who let me know that life and death is in the **power** of our very own tongue (***Proverbs 18:21)***. **Whatever we think, that is what we become.** Our thinking leads to our behaviors and what we speak into the atmosphere of our surroundings. **We become what we speak**. We maneuver according to how we think. Throughout our entire lives our choices are led from the thoughts that run across our minds every day. Our mind is how decisions are made. Here are several illustrations.

Turn the page!!!!

Getting in Where We Fit

We all wanted someone to either love us or like us, or to be a **part of something**. No one ever wants to feel like an outsider. No one ever wants to feel alone, so we do anything to fit in even if it means not being ourselves. When I think of it now, being accepted was something I highly struggled with. I was this goodie two shoes, which was what my family always called me, and a teacher's pet. Hey, I wasn't aware that being smart, pretty, and loving to learn were bad things. I even felt guilty about being pretty. People actually made me feel bad about how I looked.

So confusion set in my mind, and I felt bad because I became an outsider. People were always talking to me about how I thought I knew everything and how I was always trying to be someone's mom. In my mind **I just wanted the best**

for them. I was just trying to share with them the core values that I learned growing up. I never let anyone know that what they were saying truly did affect me on the inside. **So, I didn't want to be different anymore**; I wanted to be the same as everyone else.

Although I had a little bit of myself still intact, I started cussing, I stopped doing my work in school to the best of my ability, and after my first fight I started being a slight bully. Not to the point that I would just fight—I picked on those who picked on others. As crazy as this sounds, we all look for acceptance in some way until we are titled with the phrase "birds of a feature flock together."

I grew up always caring what others thought, but I suppose it concerned the right situations at times. Even as adults, many people still look for that acceptance from someone, whether it's from peers, family, work, etc. **But being different isn't a problem if you're being who you are.** I encourage you to get to know **who you are in Christ**. People crucify people for not being like them or following the crowd, but that only shows our own self-issues. The bible questions those to say, Isaiah 5:20: " Woe to those who call evil good and good evil." We are backwards as a people to think that doing well is evil and evil is good. When I truly came to the Lord after my long life of voids and missing pieces—finally becoming exhausted by pleasing everyone else—**with the push of God I stopped**

the life of emptiness.

I used to drink heavily before and after the age of twenty-one when I lost my virginity; it was when I truly **cracked** from peer pressure and told myself I didn't care anymore. In my mind I wanted to see what other women were going through. For two years I was in a war with my mind. I became more distanced than I have ever been in my life before. **I felt like God couldn't hear me anymore** when I would talk to Him.

It was a dark and lonely feeling. My friends would tug and war with me constantly, and my life was never my own any longer. I started to be part of the fast life—it was what I thought I had to do because I completely lost myself at this point. It began an **uncontrolled** time of confusion and anger. I had done everything with my friends, party it up, there was nothing left to do. This was what everyone was doing, right? **People do the same thing every day expecting to get different results.** I felt like if I tried to live life how I wanted to live it, God would no longer grant me that happiness because He wasn't listening to me anymore.

Nothing in my own life was coming together. I felt like I was a good girl who had finally gotten back on track with my life—I graduated high school, I was musically inclined, I started going to college. But everything kept falling apart as I would hit road blocks. I thought, OK I'm not perfect—I cussed, but I was a virgin at the time. Still, I was driven to accomplish everything in my life, even though around me it was so dysfunctional. But nothing came together, so **why not live someone else's life?** My way wasn't working.

Anyway, I remember the day I told my friends I lost my virginity. The craziest thing happened. Can you believe that they seemed disappointed? Is it me or was I getting mixed messages? I couldn't believe this. After all my hard work trying to get them to understand, to be patient and wait, they looked at me in disbelief and had the nerve to say to each other that I had changed. By this time it was already too late. I developed a careless attitude and I was feeling myself. Every moral, belief, and standard that I had unbelievably went out the window. It was as if I had forgotten or something. **All of this because I wanted their approval**, their acceptance of my new character, and had been trying to let them know that now I understand.

Truth is, I didn't know what I was in for. How does one come out of a situation in which they have voluntarily placed themselves? After two years of destruction I wanted to die from the things I had experienced. **I couldn't see myself anymore—who was the girl I had become?** There wasn't any point in living. It was like I had no control. So I spent nights **pleading** to the highest God for His mercy and grace and most of all **His forgiveness**. I knew that it wasn't going to happen in one day toward my recovery, but I had to start somewhere. I couldn't let the guys I had become one with leave the count of one of my hands. It took the strength of God and prayers of my family.

The thing about God is that **He is a forgiving God.** The bible says that when you sin against Him to repent and turn from your ways, then God because He's forgiving will cast your sins into the sea of forgetfulness (Micah 7:19). This means your sin is put away, but at a price—give up your own ways. **He is worth it and His ways are better than ours.** God knows when you are truly tired from what you have been doing. I was in need of a word so bad. The moral of this story is that **I was found**, and all because I thought I needed to be how others wanted me to be. I let their lives become my reality. I let it become my lifestyle and that became me, but I finally stopped letting others dictate my life. Most people don't know God, and if you don't **He's worth getting to know.** I was fortunate enough to have Him be part of my life since I was a child. I was called the preacher's kid and I was considered a hypocrite or backslider during my years away from God.

In this life we fight with two worlds—the right and the wrong. All of our lives we are **searching for something** to be a part of because we didn't necessarily have that in our homes. They say that we are a product of our environment.

How did we know that we wanted acceptance? **We just wanted someone to call friend**. We wanted that loyalty, someone to trust, someone to lean on, and someone who could identify with ourselves even if it meant losing who we are. We'd rather be on the inside and not the outside. **No one likes to be alone**. The devil, known as the enemy, plays these things against our minds throughout our childhood to adulthood to keep us in a vicious cycle. The bible says that he comes to steal, kill and destroy (John 10:10), and those are the very things he sets out to accomplish. He taps into our emotions and leads our thinking toward what could possibly harm us. Have you ever tried to compare and contrast something in your mind? Or even thought of something and it leads with an action? Well that's what the devil uses to take us out. If he can alter your thoughts about yourself to make you think less of yourself, to make you feel alone, to make you feel you will never get anywhere, or in my case, to think God would never love you or forgive you, then the devil can destroy you. I made up my mind later that **I wanted to be who God desired me to be** and not what man desired me to be, but the question at the time was how.

Turn the page!!!!

I̶NSECURITIES

We all face insecurities constantly running through our thoughts. Some don't like to admit these deep uncomfortable feelings about ourselves. We often question things concerning our weight class, whether we are too skinny or too big. **We compare ourselves to others**, wondering what would it take to look as good as that person? Or why weren't we genetically gifted with the right assets, weight in the right places? And some of us go beyond ourselves to even starve ourselves and eat less because our workout plans aren't working fast enough for us. **Our insecurities lead us to sabotage** others because we don't like others looking or doing better than ourselves. I remember my moments of insecurities, and every now and then things may pop up in my mind, but you have to **cast those things down**.

My constant battle was my appearance. I hated the way that I looked and the way clothes looked on me. I was just so skinny. So to hide what most called a boyish shape, I would tie my shirt around my waist and think to myself, man I wish I had some curves. Unbelievable. I was wearing bigger shirts and a pair of shorts under my pants to feel thicker and more comfortable to make myself feel better. That was my way of coping. **No one even knew** and I was happy with that. Growing up, my siblings also talked about my head and said I resembled Tweety Bird, who was also my favorite stuffed animal, and that my forehead was big. Boy did I have some major self-confidence issues, even though they were joking.

Through all these hiding issues, at least everyone thought I was pretty. I just never saw what it was that everyone else saw. I used to think nothing was appealing to the eye. I only felt that boost of confidence because I constantly heard I was pretty, which sometimes made me annoyed. When I was at home I didn't see what everyone else had tried to make it important for me to know. I felt I had a big head with big lips that I tried to mask with lip liner. I mean, everyone else's lips were small. I was straight up and down like a boy—who would think I was cute? The only thing I kept telling myself was that I had a six pack (joking), and they say my face is pretty. Now that I have become comfortable in my own skin

I have realized a lot about myself. I ended up gaining the weight I wanted. **Who's ever really satisfied?**

I remember growing up modeling, I thought that I was enough and I had something unique. I tried out for *America's Next Top Model* five times and was never picked, which made me discouraged for years. I replaced my pain with tattoos and partially with that weight gain. **I gave up hoping** that I would be given that chance. The same goes for singing, etc. After years and years of trying to put myself out there nothing came together. I never understood why. Did I not have enough drive as I thought? I was putting myself out there. The burning question for me though, is this: am I taking enough of a risk to make those things really happen? **Don't let time or repeated rejections stop you.**

Although it took me until my twenties, I realized I was decent and that **everyone has flaws**. Being in my twenties, I began to understand by the word of God that **having insecurities leads to dangers within your character** and with others. The bible talks about getting rid of envy, strife, jealousy and more. A lot of us run into these problems because we see something that another person has and so we admire it. Sometimes admiring something turns into something bigger and more complex. Having such things in your heart is **poison to the soul** and becomes corruptible—it can eat you from the inside out.

We have the power to defeat our insecurities before they develop into something more. It's understandable that some things are programmed into our minds to make us think certain things, like we have to look, act and feel the way society tells us. If we learn the true definition of who we are we can accept ourselves, and **the only way to find our identity is through Jesus Christ**. Every day we have to overcome our insecurities because they cause us to fear. God has not given us the spirit of fear but one of power, love and a sound mind. **God provides us with peace**. The peace He provides surpasses all understanding, and He promises to give those who are His more peace.

I encourage you to **fight off the enemy** trying to use your emotions to create insecurities. **We all have something to contribute to the world, we just have to tap in to what it is.** I love my body—I look like who I am and I no longer have those insecurities. I even lost the weight that I gained to be comfortable in my own skin. Crazy, I know. I realized that being thicker really wasn't what I wanted—it's what the world wanted and my loss of confidence wanted, but I was more comfortable being thin. The most important thing is for you to like and love you first.

> *For I know the thought that I think toward you, saith the Lord, thoughts of peace, and not of evil,*

to give you an expected end.
Jeremiah 29:11

God never starts anything without finishing it.

Turn the page!!!!

Fear

By definition, fear means an unpleasant emotion caused by the belief that someone or something is dangerous, likely to cause pain or threat. Now if you ask me, I don't think that expressing yourself and coming into what you're called to do is meant to cause you harm or put you in pain. There is no threat in **progressing forward**. For some reason we easily become afraid of people. We fear how they feel or what they think of us. Remember that you are one of many keys to affect change in your community. **It starts with you**. Don't allow the devil to use fear as a distraction to keep you quiet when you are an asset to a movement of change.

I've known these feelings firsthand because I have grown up with the excuse of being shy when there were so many things inside me I wanted to express. If only I could let you inside my head. I truly feared standing in front of people or being in the spotlight. Now, it was easy if I didn't say anything—I could bust out a dance in a minute or sing in a group. That wasn't a problem at all. But getting up in front of people all by myself was another story. I would get so nervous and flushed that I would start sweating, which led to a headache. I was fortunate to be able to get through these times by praying really hard to God, asking that He would lead me as I ministered. Whatever way that I was speaking, whether it was praying in front of people, singing, doing a project, doing a play or even a poem, I had to ask Christ to enter in and take over because **I couldn't do it myself**. It's so important to die to yourself when you get in front of people, or even when you are speaking to people, because you want to provoke change and transformations of the mind. You want to be able to be broken enough to feel the hearts of others. **Romans 12:15** explains this. Have compassion!

Even in relationships with people, I have my own reservations because of past hurt and being taken advantage of. Oftentimes I fear that no one will be as open and genuine as I am to them, so I fear getting close to people. I am slowly overcoming this, and realizing that no matter how things pan out in any situation, you can't allow fear to poison your character and make you become less effective. **Tell your story. Don't be afraid.**

Fear keeps many of us in bondage. Its restraints keep us confined and unable to produce. Maybe I am the only one who has experienced this. Fear makes excuses to keep you stagnant and keeps you from fulfilling your purpose. **Proverbs 18:21** says, "Death and life are in the power of the tongue: and they that love it shall eat the fruit thereof." Like I am sure you have heard before, if you speak and tell yourself that you're unable to do something, or you speak negative things in general, those become present in your life and vice versa.

Second Timothy 1:7 states: "God hath not given us the spirit of fear; but of power, and of love, and of a sound mind."

This woman named Ginny told me this recently when I told her that I was nervous to read my poem in front of people. It was the launch of my brother's Dear Poetry event named "Release the Joy," and I was first up. She told me, "Don't look at it as people staring at you making judgements. Look at it as you having a **God-giving message** to share with them that will help change their lives or perspective." Now those weren't her exact words, but they are close. It was so simple but so meaningful, and it gave me courage to understand that people are there to receive and celebrate with you. Their ear is open to gain insight or knowledge about what God is saying through you. Take that stand to **embrace your fears and turn them into something that would release greatness inside of you.**

My Poem from that night:
August 15, 2015 (My birthday)

Look Beneath

If they can just get past this phase,
and look beneath the surface

They would see my true rhythm comes from
being selfless

A melody my heart loves to keep,
For what is this life without the father's Heartbeat

See oftentimes people shelter one with words
that are made hollow

And from 10 secs of you making up my identity
for me comes your labels without knowing me

Words like being selfish, prideful, develops
lovers of themselves reprobated

Now see that doesn't define me

Well did you know that Jesus was transfigured,
changing and radiant in appearance?

And yet they still threw stones denying his very existence

How can someone so wonderful be denied, calling his work wrong when his word is right?

See the compliments are nice but don't try to put inside of a box filled with your assumptions and thoughts that I'm just………..this surface….

No don't get twisted,

This is just my armor, handcrafted by the father above; he just added some details that formed me From the dust, but I, promise I had nothing to do with it

Try not to dwell in the flesh,

For I rather you judge me by my suit then take ownership of what God has done.

Take your eyes off this flesh.

For I believe the ultimate test lies within your security

Because beauty is in the eye of the beholder, it's not measured by how you compare yourself

No one should ever assume, fear, attack or even single someone out for their own gain.

If we say we represent the father in Heaven, the most high, the lord of all and the kings of Kings.

So let me reintroduce myself,
Hi my name is Tamar and I am a woman of God.

It's so important to be lowly on the inside and out. I wrote this poem because people always identified me as the pretty or beautiful girl. There are only a few who know me for my **beauty on the inside**. My image sometimes made me afraid to talk to people or approach them. In my mind I automatically felt that there would be some negative reaction or that they would portray me to be some way that I wasn't. In some ways I have adapted to my image; I have a sense of confidence about who I am and how I look. I never try to portray myself as self-entitled or even appear as if I am better.

Although I may feel this way, **God is not done with me yet**. In the year 2015 I started to break out really bad and get spots all over my face. Can I tell you that I seriously began to freak out and even cry about it? I began asking the Lord **why this was happening and what had I done**. I've been nice to people. Is there something you're trying to show me, and if so could you do it another way? Why my skin, Lord? I have a fashion show to do. Right! I started to rebuke word-spoken curses against my appearance and any naysayers. I started rebuking unbalances and bacteria in my skin that may be there. I was afraid to go to the gym to show my face. I even bought a hat to hide myself, not wanting anyone to look at me. My confidence was shot, OK.

I'm not a fan of makeup, so the fact that I now had to wear makeup to work every day defeated me. I can say that

I take pride in healthy-looking skin and I like to keep mine clear. Was there something wrong with that? Nothing I was putting on my skin sped up my skin's process of clearing up. I decided to give up and embrace it. I looked odd, and you could tell that my skin wasn't meant to break out like it did. I didn't understand. I started walking around with my head down because I knew people might be looking at me. My family members told me that I didn't even look like myself. I agreed. They told me that it may be more of a spiritual thing. Although I felt I wasn't doing anything wrong—but could it be a possibility that **God is still cleaning up my character?** I am not sure. What I can tell you about this is that if there is any pride or too much pride in myself concerning my appearance, I am dying to myself again. I have died to myself even more, and I die to my outer-self daily. Also be sure to rebuke witchcraft and naysayers. I say this to say:

It's the inside that matters. We do so much work on the outside and don't even take care of the inside like we should. Continue to work on your inner man because your flesh is what's going to wither away, but how have you made a positive effect?

Turn the page! Always be humble and lowly. Come against hind-minded agendas and cast them down when they arise in your mind, no one has arrived!

Love vs. *Lust*

I found out that a lot of people confuse the meanings of love and lust. We all look for love mainly from fairytales imagined from what we are taught or have seen in our homes. We watched all the romantic movies and have seen all the dreamy plays, and we think to ourselves: **that's the kind of love I want.** The type of love that sweeps us off our feet and everything goes well. That love where we would smile and laugh every day. How disappointing when we find out that **love is far more than that**. We have the definition of love so messed up that it leads to misuse and high divorce rates. I always felt like I knew the true definition of love, remembering how I wrote it in a poem at a young age. The odd thing was I wasn't wrong. It was the experience behind what I had written that I was missing. People think that love is just that first feeling that we feel, and a lot of us misuse it to get what we want. A lot of times I see people set themselves up for failure of love by looking in all the wrong places. **In all reality, what we feel is lust.**

Lust is that simulating, enticing feeling that attracts us to another person. It's **that attention that we are missing** and it urges us to find it by any means. As I stated before, many of us lack certain things in our homes, and **the biggest thing lacking is love**. So we begin this journey of lust. Lust is not just sexual if that's what you're thinking. It's the burning desire of wanting something, that craving that leads to addiction. It's the use of that desire to fill void as a replacement. **We crave the things we didn't have, in turn substituting them for something that's nothing close to what we set out to do in the beginning.** Lust has become the norm in cultures today. It causes us to jump in and out of relationships and make choices that are not clearly thought out.

Going through the things that I faced caused me to know in-depth the difference between love and lust. I, like many others, had the perception of a fairytale love. That love was just this magical feeling and white fence, with the phenomenal house with no problems or issues and everything that I painted it to be. My order and my way. I'm not saying those material things are impossible—no they are not. Those things are within reach, but I learned that they won't make you happy. My point is, **even when you have everything, if love isn't there then in most cases it won't last.** I knew that love was happiness and I knew that love lasted if it was true. I also found out that no one was looking for it. No one wanted the kind of love that was much more than words, the kind that included actions also. That type of love that separates you from everyone else. The type of love that would battle with you. I had the mentality to love hard—that love was easy to find and everyone was full of it. I never factored in that other person's scarring or lack of knowledge of love. **I understood that love was the way God loves**. Something that was pure and beautiful and gentle and everything, that **no one can separate you from it**.

    I wanted to find that, but in my years growing up it was all about games and intimacy with no emotions. Seeing that it was absent in many people, I grew cold toward individuals, never to become attached. I loved God, well at least to my understanding at the time. I loved to give, but if any were to try and tap into my emotions you would think they didn't exist. **Being in the Lord has taught me so much about love that I was recreated.** I learned that **love is sacrifice** and that there are ups and downs. I would have moments when I would tell God that I loved, and I questioned Him as to why things were not coming together. I would preach His word and tell them that they needed to get their lives together and come to church. It took me growth and wisdom to understand that I was living a double standard lifestyle. How much did I love God by telling people to follow Him, but living the same way they did? I understood later that **I had to separate myself from my old habits to really understand love**. If I loved God the way that I said that I did, then why was I still doing all the things I was doing and calling it holy? I'm talking everything from my love life to my lifestyle. **Sure I knew what love was, but I wasn't living in love**. There are so many things that factor into love that I wasn't aware of. **Love is painful** just as much as it brings you happiness. A lot of people thrive off of conditional love, which is temporary. It says that I can only love you for a season when you make me feel a certain way. It requires you to be happy all the time, and if someone slips up then it's easy for you to separate yourself from that person or something.

When you understand the love of God and what God has done by love then you will know how to love yourself and others. No one can make you happy or satisfied or feel loved, but I know a God who loves **past my faults** and mishaps. In order to know love and understand how to live in the order of love, you have to erase from your mind everything that you thought it was. **Love isn't what you think it should be like** or the emotion of it. I stress that because if you are depending on someone to keep your feelings going then I encourage you to **depend on God and not on man**. Love comes from you embracing the love that's from Christ, and **then you can know love, feel love and give love**. That is what makes you complete, the in-depth relationship with God.

Covenant love, or better yet love in a marriage between a man and woman, takes the two individuals knowing exactly what they want and where they are going. The individuals have to know the importance of covenant and faithfulness. You have to know that you're not missing out on anything and that **when you have true love you won't risk it for meaningless moments**. Sometimes a man and a woman can be very selfish because we are only used to dealing with ourselves our entire lives. When you **truly** love, become open, make that person your best friend, and treat them like you would treat yourself, then you can be outside yourself and understand why you would never hurt that person. **It's partnership.** Most people usually don't get it because we allow small things to break us. Sorry, but I cannot discuss love between two un-married individuals because I believe the full expression of love comes when the two are joined in matrimony and then tested with trials and tribulation. I mean, if you love someone that much why not make them your husband or wife? I believe that trying to live or cohabit and exist together is the wrong way of doing things. This may offend people, but please respect the fact that I am a woman of God and I believe solely in what the word says.

I haven't always been a true Christian, nor have I gone according to the word. **I am imperfect and strive to mature every day.** I have had the experience of giving myself away weeks after the age of twenty-one, and at twenty-three I realized that I was misusing my value and I fell in love with this guy. From that point I started living my life celibate and I assured this man that if he desired to be with me then the only way to do that was to **give our life to Christ**. We joined a church and started living out life for Christ.

OK, wait a minute! Before I go further, I want to encourage you to pay close attention to the signs whether they are good or bad. **It's easy to be blind to love** believing that you made all the right moves, especially with faith.

Back to this guy. I fell in love with him and he strived hard to be everything that he needed to be for me. He had the intention to be better and live a Godly lifestyle. I do sincerely believe that he was in love with me as well, but the ultimate issue was he didn't know how to love me—he didn't understand what real love takes. He was a super nice guy to everyone else and to me as well most of the time. We had our battles. His heart was what drew me in; he had potential and was willing. (Determining where you are in your walk will let you know if it is right with God or not.) To get to the point, he became my husband. My husband had many struggles in his life that affected him, and he struggled to let go of his past habits and self and to be a complete husband. I am not writing this to bash my husband, but only to encourage those who may feel love to know that **sometimes God wants us to give it completely to Him.**

My marriage had its trouble from the start. There was always backlash about me not being with him and him not being it for me. No one understood the reasons why I fell for him or continue to strive for a better life with him. My husband, due to his past and some other things that seem to linger unknown, got deported. I want to be completely transparent with you. Through most of our relationship people would refer to it as questionable. I had really accepted things I normally wouldn't have… **Everyone is different**…

He spent most of his time in jail on the road of trying to become a better person (which is his testimony to tell to people). When I met him he had some things going on that I wasn't completely aware of. I had talked to him about doing the right things to clean up his life, and of course none of the people he associated himself with had liked his road of transformation. After the first couple of months I found out that he was violating his probation and never reporting in. Needless to say, they put him on house arrest, and to my surprise he violated that and landed himself in jail. Now, a normal person would say leave him alone and **RUN** for your life. I cannot tell you clearly now whether it was my emotions or Godly belief that made me believe I was meant to stick it out with him, but it was mostly **faith**. At that moment it was clear.

So I did. I watched him grow after he had gone in for two years, but there were still things he couldn't break. He had troubles of dying to himself. He had troubles with treating me like a woman and acknowledging me as such. He made me feel last at times, but I don't think he was aware of it. My husband, like many others, was **a product of his environment**. It's the environment where society tells you to play games with each other in the process of hurting one another's feelings. In a sense he acted like he was playing me off and he wasn't able to give me his full self or heart. He never let me in for some reason, and he hid a lot of things from me. I didn't understand why he didn't see how much I loved him and how much I was fighting for him. Although there were these problems, he still was my best friend. **When we were good, we were good, and when we were bad, we were bad**, lol! Bless his heart. He is a good person.

I wanted the best for my husband and every day I aimed to push him to do better by **encouragement**. If you were to hear it from him he would say a lot of the things he did were because he wanted to provide for me. I told my husband that if we just relied on God then we would be fine. My husband didn't like that I was the one making the money for us at the time because he wanted to be the man, which is fine. I believe that got to him. He didn't realize that I understood the season he was in to get back on his feet. Yes, I was pushing and pushing—it was getting stressful because everyone's eyes were on us. He felt the pressure and I did too, so we argued. Am I going to tell you that I was perfect? No, I am not. I began to get frustrated with how I was treated, although I was sacrificing things for him. We fought and there was a lot of name calling and distrust—so draining. **Never tear each other down when you are down. You leave wounds and a mindset that potentially may struggle to become renewed**.

When the pressure was on, sometimes he would slack finding a job. That would worry me because he isn't the type who wants to work for anyone, seeing that he came from the fast life. I tried to explain to him that we needed to start somewhere. By the end of all these hardships, here I am in Christ and struggling in my heart. **My heart was hurting and God was tugging me.**

The important thing to remember is no matter how disappointed you get with your spouse, you still need to speak the **language of love** and build him or her up. I had my troubles as well—from where we started I did not fully trust him in making decisions, and I didn't fully trust to leave him by himself at times. I even didn't like when he spoke. This sounds terrible, I know. I truly, deeply loved him, but our vision together wasn't aligned completely right. You must be **transparent** with your spouse and not misleading—that leads to more issues, trust me. You have to learn to **give up your independent eyes**. Our marriage felt like competition. Please **honor** each other, don't compete. I thought I was supposed to fight. Take note that just because someone has potential or is a good guy, ultimately that doesn't mean they are the person you are meant to wed. **God gives us signs; we just have to open our eyes to see them past ourselves.**

One day I was at work and I was calling my husband, who was just my fiancé at the time, and I never got a response. All I knew was that he went to a bible study with the men at church. I received a phone call at eleven o'clock letting me know that he was back in jail. My entire world became void. Disappointments and confusion began to fill my mind and soul. I even began to be angry and so hurt because he knew what we were battling. People were already against us and we were on a rocky level, but I continued to stay because of **my faith in us and the belief that God said he was my husband.** He was in jail for a year and this time I couldn't get him out of it. I just kept praying and praying. He went back and forth to court and at the end it resulted in him getting deported. I was so destroyed but **I stuck by him**.

The church I had attended at the time kind of shook their heads at me, and asked me out of the church for reasons that are without understanding. They told me that I wasn't happy there, when I was kind. I had to fight so much at that time. I was sold out for Christ, singing in the worship group, praying constantly, and feeling **the fire of God** through my veins. **I just wanted to serve the Lord** with my whole heart. Be mindful that all these things don't determine if you're a true Christian. Your relationship with Christ does. But as I learned, in every church there are always things going on because like you, others are coming to be **transformed**.

They said things to me that hurt me, but still I loved them and took it until they asked me to leave indirectly. See, my thoughts were **if Jesus could withstand, then with his strength I was able to as well**. I felt like the church was too focused on petty things and not the growth in character in Christ. Maybe I misunderstood some things, but we as a body have to be careful when making judgements and assumptions about other people. That should never be done. I know that maybe deep down they possibly wanted what was best for me. If it could have been shown differently I would have understood. There was just so much going on that didn't add up. I truly cared for the people at this church and I was in agreement with the vision there. It's unfortunate. I love them still and we later reconciled, and I will always be in support of them.

AS A BODY OF CHRIST

We are there to grow, uplift and show the love of Christ, and help each other or be an aid for Christ to live a holy lifestyle. Murmuring and complaints and gossip are where many fail and have others going backward. **Going backward isn't worth it, but being right with God is.** I learned that we have to put on our **Armor** and trust in Christ because **no man can you trust**. This means to be careful putting your all in man without the knowledge of knowing that he or she is man. Man makes mistakes, will hurt and disappoint you. Just please don't allow those things to guide you away from the bigger picture, which is Christ and the will of God. The important thing from all of this is to **forgive, so that your heart may be settled**. Nothing held in your heart is ever worth it. Don't let harbored pain or grudges hold you back from progress or your future.

BACK TO THE STORY

Well, I didn't go back to the church, but I did go to Africa where my husband was deported. I needed to know for myself. I was so certain that God said **yes**. At first it was rough, he still had things going on, but we shared the most **amazing moments in Christ**. We went to church every day and deliverance started to take place. We prayed together and I saw **doors starting to open in the spiritual realm**. Even he began to pray, but he still had old flaws that followed him. With this said, I had married him when I got to Africa, which was against my parents and my family. In Africa they treated us with the most respect, like we were royals.

It wasn't until my last two weeks of being there that my husband started to change in character, letting the old self or mindset go. Unfortunately, it wasn't enough time. I left to go back to Ohio and things immediately started to shift. What we had grown to have fell off, and he reverted back into his old habits and other things that were unwise. This resulted in filing for a divorce. See, I asked the Father what it was that I should do in this situation, and although the decision was tough, I knew that **He led me to let it go**. There were a lot of things going on that I haven't disclosed, but my heart was overwhelmed and I was dying emotionally and spiritually.

I fell apart. My spiritual life began to die inside. My intense prayers with God began to be **talks with Christ** every chance I got, and songs to Him here and there. I lost my prayer life. I was afraid to go to any church because the word that I needed I couldn't find, and **I was numb to God**. There was one woman who has a heart for Christ—I met her when she came into the salon and I started doing her hair—and God by purpose led me to go to the church where she and her husband pastor together. Through her words from God, a lot of pain broke off of me and I was able to release everything I was harboring. (Thank you, Prophetess Perry, woman of God.) I cried out every night. **In a way I resented God, as we always do when we can't understand, and I couldn't hear his voice.** I often looked down on myself, feeling useless to God because there wasn't anything that I was doing for Him, or ministering for Him. I just found myself not having words, except for, "Sorry if I disappointed you" or, "Help me," etc. I just wanted to look like the person God saw me as. I just couldn't comprehend how this was the outcome after I had done well and my hands had been clean.

My husband told me that he loved me and we were progressing. My thoughts were now, *I look foolish to have had faith and belief that God can change things around.* I felt like it was entirely my fault because maybe I was missing the signs (and I was missing them). But how can you miss the signs when you know the love between two people was real? How could this happen. My mind told me that everyone was right and now I couldn't even show my face.

The most beautiful thing that I was able to experience in this process was **forgiveness**. All the things that took place I was able to look at in newness. **My prayers and talks and healing with Christ gave me the ability to love, and although I felt like I was nobody to God, I continued to pursue Him**. God gave me the ability to love unconditionally with joy. I was able to tell my ex-husband that everything was OK. That he didn't have to feel guilty about anything that took place and that I see him as a new person. I even pray for him and his future endeavors, even his future wife. I think he will be a great person when God takes ahold of his heart completely. He has so much promise. I feel the same way about my old church. I truly love them as Christ does. **Forgiveness is the key and your greatest weapon of peace**

to regaining joy.

Your ability to see someone as a new person is the source of your strength that comes from God in your weakness. I was able to love him past his mistakes once I understood his struggles and once I gave everything to God this time, for real. I began to become more secure with myself and understand that no matter what, the relationship set apart with Christ is **THE** most important. You have to be one with the Lord regardless. Get in relationship with God. **He wants to hear your voice so He can direct you.** I understand that I wasn't hearing as I thought.

I keep feeling like the spirit of the Lord is saying to me that my marriage and its failures have nothing to do with anyone. Not my family, nor the church, etc., because my heart was in the right place and what we shared was true. We were only meant to cross paths for a season. It's not even his fault. The main thing is that **I made an impact in his life by the ushering of the Holy Spirit.** I can say that he was worth standing up for; he was worth loving even if it was for a moment. I knew his heart. It just happened that we were in different seasons of our lives. This is all for **growing**. I pray the best for his life. My circumstances may be different than others'. I don't believe in divorce and I never thought it would happen. However, he is in Africa and I am in America and I know that letting go was the right thing to do. It freed not only me but him as well, especially because he lived his own life in Africa. He needed to grow for him and I didn't want him to feel guilty. We just truly weren't ready and thought we were able to be stronger. To avoid the weaknesses of man I knew the Lord was telling me to separate. Sorry if it sounds contradictory.

I constantly battled with myself after that season, sometimes saying that this could have been avoided. I have shamed myself. **Why me?**

One would think that my relationship with Christ was dependent upon the relationships I had with people. That's not it. Going through church hurt, and love hurt, and having faith through all these things takes a toll on you like I never thought before. My faith told me that **there was nothing impossible in Christ**, and if I fervently kept praying then why wouldn't things work together for the good? It's what He says in the word, but that was my own understanding. I often looked back and realized that maybe there had been doubt all along, but I still had and needed to experience the **love** I had for him. It was my way of overcoming my fears.

What can I tell you about all this? I can tell you that although it seems like my faith failed me and I am so destroyed inside, **keep fighting for Christ**. I even stopped talking with God, even though maybe there was another route or plan for me. Even though I was afraid to pray to Him at times because

I didn't know what to ask for, I tried anyways, because I have experienced Christ through me and all that He has been in my life. **There is nothing more that I desire, but Him.** I love God so deeply that it hurts that there wasn't anything I could have done for Him, or that my words were limited to Him because I didn't know what to say. I felt unworthy and ineffective. When pain tried to take me away from God I couldn't go because **there isn't anything I want from sin, nor can it offer anything to me. God is far more than that to me.** I know that deep down I am in love with God; I was just so unaware of what He wanted me to do.

So my option isn't to go back to a worldly, sinful lifestyle just because I have gone through these things. I'd rather have a boring lifestyle than to go through or live a cycle of a lifestyle that keeps me going nowhere, and will ultimately lead me to death in my walk with Christ. BY the way, **the Christian lifestyle isn't boring!**

What I have come from in my past life I will never desire to revisit. Now I am in a place to explore myself and Christ within me. I practice to position myself to always be used by God as a servant for **His glory.**

HOWEVER...

I can't sit here and tell you that it's easy to get through all this stuff, but I am saying that **God is worth the wait** and He will work in your situation. Let God put the pieces together and every day it will get better—the **strength** of the Lord directs.

Increased prayer life and worship is our best connection. I enjoy singing to God and being in His presence.

Isn't it so funny how we can blame ourselves? That's what the **enemy** uses to keep us down. Let go of your past pain and regrets for the sake of your future. I have and you can.

No one ever said that it would be easy to **overcome,** or that everything would line up right away as quickly as you thought it would. Through my unawareness, I can only say to others to be patient and keep fighting for Christ because

He fights for you. Avoid temptations and sinful lust. **Stay strong** in your prayer life regardless of your setbacks and disappointments. Sometimes just when we feel like giving up, it's around the time God shows up. He is worth serving and giving your life to. In the hardest of battles your **prayer activates His strength** and helping hand to you. I speak life not just to you, but also to myself. God is **everything** you're looking for. He is worth getting to know. Overall, it's important to have singleness with God before any relationship because Christ is who makes us entire or whole, not man. **The Joy of the Lord is your strength**. My encouragement is to continue to fight even when you feel alone. It is easy to have a one-track mind. When you are married, God has to be the center of both of you; He guides us to what to do. You have the ability in Christ together to take down anything the devil throws at you. **Unity!**

The love you're looking for is in Christ and **in Him you will find everything**. Trust me, as I'm on my Journey. Love is God and it's that love, when it's according to God's plan for you, that will last till eternal life.

Listen! At least now I know how to be wifey if I do get married again, lol. Who knows! Not really worried about that right now. Focus on God, singles, and He will find you and be OK with getting to know you while you are waiting if you desire a husband or wife. **God's got you!**

Oh yeah, my ex-husband and I. We have respect for each other and we are friends. I wish him all the best!

Let's Shift.

TRIALS AND TRIBULATIONS

Like many others, as you have noticed from what you have already read, I faced and endured a lot of trials. One of my trials that tends to have an effect on me is having financial stability and making sure I maintained it. Sounds familiar! I have always worked very hard, but somehow I chose a line of work that allowed me to get paid minimum wage. **God always made a way** and He always supplied my needs. I knew He was **calling** me higher, but I couldn't produce it as soon as I expected it and so I questioned. I had no understanding. I would ask God every year of my life, how was it that people were able to put their pieces together and upstart their lives? **What was I missing?** My brother told me that I would just have to do it and not think so much about it. For me that sounds easier said than done. It was like I had all the information and the vision in my mind, but I couldn't release it to manifest. How desperate or **passionate for change** do you have to be for manifestation to start happening in your life? I'm talking about the desperation that results in your members (hands) beginning to work out your situation to produce an outcome **(Psalms 128:2). Do you really want it to happen?**

Trials come so unexpectedly sometimes and we aren't even prepared. As I go through mine with personal or job-related aspects on the mind, I notice that I am gaining **experience** to be able to relate or deliver a testimony to someone in a similar situation. **Trials are meant to make you stronger; do not let them break you or stagnate you.** I have faced many ups and downs in my life in plenty of areas. I can humbly tell you that **I am flawed**. We are all flawed in some area or areas, but there is hope and we can change how we respond to our tribulation. Though I don't do what people consider big sin—drinking, clubbing, fornication, etc.—I often die to myself daily in my character. The ability to overcome yourself when your flesh tries to puff up is important. It is a fatal thing. To think higher causes you to fall greatly. True faith use was a trial for me.

> Therefore being justified by faith, we have peace with God through our Lord Jesus Christ: By whom

also we have access by faith into this grace wherein we stand, and rejoice in hope of the glory of God. And not only so, but we glory in tribulations also: Knowing that tribulation worked patience and patience, experience, and experience hope.
Romans 5:2-3

Let's all be on the road and journey to build ourselves in faith every day—**take that leap of faith with me**. I'm asking the Lord that He may **strengthen** me, and you as well, to embark on these visions that He placed before us that they may **manifest** in the natural world. I also pray that no weapon formed against them shall prosper and that we will use our words and that they will be life to us to move us forward, in Jesus' name. **Amen.**

Heartfelt

Drowning, broken, hidden, sharp poundings
All factor into the world
Pain ripped, stiff, unclear, alone
Detached I fear, injured, wounded
Lord I'm begging that you keep me strong
Focused, so forgive me that I don't lose my words, hopeless
Love, pain, Jesus is this what you felt so much to endure
Don't let me lose my keys, worship, praise, prayer
My sound allows me to fight through the storms
As the enemy tries to blind me,
I know true love will return even better than before
Keep me leveled patient and strong.
I am strong and desperate for you, through my heartache I still trust you
My Lord, My savior. I love you!

Faith Fighting

This is challenging because sometimes you may get in situations where your faith will almost attempt to waver. We often ask questions and blame God when we are placed in these circumstances. Those constant questions about things we don't have understanding to know. We tend to ask God why or how could this happen when an outcome is different than what we expected. I mean, we prayed and maybe fasted and we believed. **What could go wrong?**

I had to fight with these on many occasions. I believe it's so important to hear the **voice of God**. As I stated before, my biggest fight with faith was the direction of my life and all that was involved in it. It's hard to focus on your faith when certain things pull or attempt to shake you from it. **Your faith is lifelong**; it's not an experience you encounter.

We have to continue to speak what we believe no matter if it happens today or tomorrow.

I don't know about you, but I was the type to feel as if I had been waiting so long. I prayed the same prayer every day and even felt like I was obedient. I mean, how were there no manifestations of my actions? **Lack of understanding**! You know how when people are speaking into your life and you're just super excited and all in the spirit like, "Yes, Lord, I receive it." And your hands are all raised like, "That's my confirmation, Lord, I knew you said it." I don't know about you, but every day I was looking for that **confirmation** and reciting it to myself like I knew it was going to happen. After a while I had gotten weary of reciting it to myself like, "Lord, what's happened?" Jesus states, **"Is not faith the substance of things hoped for and the evidence of things not seen?"** See, that's just it—as we get weary of the wait we begin to stop hoping. We begin to stop praying and start saying to ourselves, "If it was meant to happen then it will." At this point we have become discouraged. You must **keep applying your faith** and put your members to work to produce your dream. God does all the supernatural work and places you in the right places. Be present when He works things through so you can do your part. **Apply faith. Write the prayer, pray, write the plan, and then take action.**

Let's be God's workers so we can see manifestations in

our lives. **God can make anything happen**. We just have to line up with His will and everything will flow together. If you desire to partner in business, we can't be afraid to partner with each other in faith and be each other's extension to the next level. That's what we are here for. One man can't do it all by himself; **we truly need each other** whether it's in faith, praying, financial needs, or encouragement. I have learned that sometimes you have to receive encouragement in faith with those who believe, and **self-encourage** when it's not given. We should always intercede for each other so that God will give us the strength for each other. If you are doing it by yourself and you step out in faith and action, God brings forth the increase and people will be drawn to you. I have seen this happen in many lives and I am working to apply this daily. I'm not perfect! I work more to serve the kingdom of God and I am working constantly to produce what's in me—**you have to keep going against all odds**. Team up with other vision believers, those who desire to go higher. **Pray, pray, pray for strength!**

We all get weak sometimes and God is aware of our weakness. Pray that God leads you or us to those divine connections to keep one's eyes gazing upon Him.

Keep believing. It's tough at times, but faith produces action. Dedicate your time to what you believe can happen for you. Get to work! Invest time and resources into your dream. It takes you, not just faith alone. It's not about being at the same speed as others, just complete what God has placed in you. He always saves the best for last. Manifestation time.

Faith without works is dead.

This is the beginning of **Life**!

And let us not be weary and well doing: for in due season we shall reap, if we faint not.
Galatians 6:9

My continuous walk with God matures me daily. For Christ I live, for Him I die, because He turned the page! Love you all!

Revealed

Wounded by stones, stressed by the depressed and oppressed,

Trying to hide behind the disguise of the flesh.

Noticeable apparent, transparent, revealed through the eyes of the blessed.

Saying chosen by living in image of the rest, trying to get approved but denying the blood resurrect. A question must be raised, but if you can look me in the eyes and tell me that you're truly saved. Follow the leader seems problematic.

Difficulty with identity but automatic deceivable, relying upon the man seems believable, but discerning with the spirit man you can detect when the contrary tries to plug the ears, even with the chosen elect, if possible.

Be ye transformed instead, probable cause, sound sufficient, separated from death but led, by the spirit, justified by the father, consumed by the presence of righteousness, defined by the

light, creating a new existence, circumcised by the heart makes one dwelling not apart but different, hated by many,

but even the enemy comes to peace seeing the covering of the blood, impossible to touch tries to shake you but you stay steady, feared the minded and ready, faith sky rocked, reach a new level, mind-blowing with the anointing one consumed, headstrong faithfully walking in the word of the truth.

Be encouraged!

It's your turn, to turn the page!